THE

TRUANT

LOVER

FOR FIONA,
WITH DEEP
ADMIRATION
AND THANKS

X

Juliet Patterson

3/06

WINNER OF THE NIGHTBOAT POETRY PRIZE

THE

TRUANT

LOVER

Nightboat Books

Beacon, New York

2006

Library of Congress

Cataloging in Publication Data

Patterson, Juliet.

The truant lover / Juliet Patterson.

p. cm.

ISBN 0-9767185-2-9

I. Title.

PS3616.A8776T78 2006

811'.6—dc22

2005037226

Original Printing 2006

Text and cover design by Tim Roberts

CONTENTS

ACKNOWLEDGMENTS

Grateful acknowledgment is made to the following publications, where many of these poems appeared in earlier versions: *ache*, *American Letters & Commentary*, *Bellingham Review*, *Bloom*, *Conduit*, *DIAGRAM*, *Hayden's Ferry Review*, *Indiana Review*, *The Journal*, *New Orleans Review*, *Painted Bride Quarterly*, *Sonora Review*, *Three Candles*, *typo*, *Verse*, *Washington Square* and *Word for/ Word*.

Thanks to the Minnesota State Arts Board, the Jerome Foundation, the Norcroft Harmony Fund and the Anderson Center for Interdisciplinary Studies for providing me with the funds and the time to complete this work.

I did not write this book alone: thanks to Joseph Bednarik, Suzanne Heyd, Deborah Keenan, Jackie Lalley and Alex Lemon for valuable editorial assistance and support. Thanks also to the people who've sustained me: Karla Brom, Kerrie Coborn, Thor Eisentrager, Felicia Glidden, Jane Green, Sharon Jacks, Carolyn and Jim Patterson and David Wojahn.

To Kazim Ali, Jennifer Chapis, and Jen Currin of Nightboat Books, much gratitude.

To Jean Valentine for selecting the book, my enduring thanks.

To Rachel Moritz, whose love, generosity and intelligence helped this book to find itself.

Finally, not without: Barbara Cohen, Wendy Lewis, Erin Gleeson, Donna Partridge and Alexa Bradley.

FOREWORD

The Truant Lover embodies a risky, bright spirit, playful and also seeing the world and the self/ the other at a somber depth. Juliet Patterson could be working from the tradition of Lorine Niedecker, by way of Creeley, though he is not mentioned here; but the poems glance in with his kind of generosity of feeling.

This work—or play—has a quality of stillness and movement at once, and never seems to worry about being wrong. Otherwise, you feel, these poems could not have come into being.

And Juliet Patterson's poems are entirely themselves: they use time and the eye and the tongue—all the body—as thought and insight, inside and outside of history. *The Truant Lover* is a marvel.

Jean Valentine

THE

TRUANT

LOVER

NOTE

In the original, the sex of the person
at the next table is ambiguous.

The anonymous
speaker is not an imaginary

character.
The first version

was written
with the title,

"Love It More."
Loosely rhymed.

The speaker encumbered
by love. Threes, threes

& threes. Three roses
& three stems.

Red where in the whorls
petal lying in its glow,

her immaculate white bed
mounts a lonely street.

PRAYER FOR LORINE NIEDECKER

i. Lycaenidae

Egg overwinters.
Egg aquamarine.

Egg pastel green changing to ivory.
A silken girdle

the morning mirrors. In flower bud
& stem, a dominant X

body that could never be wounded,
no self in the mass,

eats words without meaning.
Later they loot.

Milk pea, lima bean.
Stream beds, wastes.

Weak, slow flyer
moving among sleepers.

Both sexes white below.
Both sexes translucent.

ii. Pieridae

The dreamer planted this field.
Forms, flames, the beating wings.

They do not beat by pain,
nor meditate the world.

Sun, forgive me if I pretend
to speak to you.

Mirror, mirror.
Yellow afternoon.

Cluttering the clover
with sudden ornament.

Several have black borders
above. Others bear delicate

pink fringes. Around which silence
lies on silence.

All around & helpless
at the edge, some have been drinking,

intimate with strangers,
where they joy, fly & whore.

iii. Papilionidae

Come, the gathering.
Fleeting cloud shadows

on the dull slopes
above the timber line, trunks

painted with molasses & beer.
Here's a world for today:

killing & not dying
fantastically, not lying.

Members breeding
on poisonous members

store the poisons
for their own defense.

The double face of leaves
is leaving across the third,

perfume of wings, dark
& curved.

HAND INSIDE

For instance, the ear of a snail.
Is that a koan? Or the canal
of a chili pepper? Or the ear of Vincent
Van Gogh covered in a kerchief & meant as gift.
Terrible was his love, thou sayest,
or beautiful. What sayest thou?
Do you hear a siren?
My lips start moving but say
nothing. Is that a moan?
Or the roof of a convertible open to a sky tossing plums?
Mourning doves pecking in the gutter.
Sounds like More! More!
Am I wrong in this?
In the world there are innumerable disturbances!
Bird song & spit, cords threaded
through trickling thunder.
The snail doesn't dream!
Inside the snail
is a snail, brains to fire.
Who needs an ear?
My hand inside
your mouth. The perfume is flowers
among crushed white stone.

OFF BERNERAY

Two hands where a train stops
in the middle of the countryside.

Smell of vetiver in an unfamiliar room,
smell of orris-root in the little closet.

The body is white. The sleeves
white, too, pushing

a bicycle. Death does not make any great
difference. The simplest act remains

immured within a thousand sealed vessels

in the blue volutes of morning sea,
rural sea.

Blue tits in the blossoming apple
tree, gulls floating like water lilies.

Smell of her bedspread.
Further nicknames.

A pink congelation of sunshine
& cold, a little simpering

laugh. I'm standing on ocean
strand, written in half.

A book is a huge cemetery
against the lemon fragrance of guelder-

roses, the last page turning.

WHO IS HER OTHER A FIGURE IN THE PICTURE ATTENDING

was first the right
eye, then left

where a field too quickly
unfolded wrong-legged

under the eye's lens

not the same wind-raised direction of crest
in reeds from reeds, the birds' hovering—

was hurry to sphere & show & end

to discover rock, scissor, felt-tip
ink, red-winged blackbirds in rain

was margin of black against margin

of shore-line, two-fold the eye
called sleeve

& cold sky reading its mineral palm

was the eye's tactic
conferring privilege on she who tends

to dissolve where cutting
blue iris & top of its stalk

inflecting the speech of the subject,
the pencil's trunk

the "you" in the lead

beneath the scissors' cutting

was a field unreeling
retinal flare

as if the house might suddenly rise to relieve

was almost loved the reed
itself reverse

of the beloved, other
instrument to bind this note

to lift the eyelid, govern & show
& end

was a made self

maybe

A NARRATIVE

Origami swans floating in the toilet.

The principles of gravity. She is talking
& talking.

A carton of owls spilling on the floor.

Eating Thai food.
Won-ton, wanton.

Everything blushing, failing, fading.

Paper birds, polls dropping.

She is talking about phone banks, hail.

Her face is a red, red seed.

She wants to grow a good rutabaga
in the burial ground.

She says happiness, happiness
& isn't satisfied.

For the poem begins because she can see
thirty-one varieties of black
in capitalism.

At a bare minimum, the clock on the wall says three.

A bowl of plum sauce bathed in light.

Swans scattered like toys.

This is obviously about a person alone.
In another version, I was her wife.

I shall be her wife.

INDEX OF FIRST LINES

ANON

Fields instress Yellow
noise

the murmuring of bees

Dear She
writes to miss you

interrupts this ground

+ Enlarges the steady-
tilled

Anon, I
am teeming

        torn

until Kansas

with the pupil, each
part of the body becoming

a tool   that the catch locks
between just-
being

& always being

Where my hands are cut
her fingers will be found

Inside

THE RIM

i.

Where the wind blew off a shingle the house
began to howl. We were composed.
At the same time, these events disturbed us,
as the house cried a meaning inseparable from its absence.
Philosophers concurred: the long habit of living
indisposeth us to dying. These thoughts fall apart when you think
them. Every hunting, hungering lover is half
a knucklebone, the mouth its first darkness. If you listen
closely, you can hear termites beating heads
against the floor in the dark, sand falling on paper, an orchestra
of trapdoors.

Nearby: the sleeping brain unmonitored,
exhausted history. You can hear the ocean's second,
second sound. Below: we stroke linen sheets & dream.
The refrigerator bows, gives milk.
The soul is eternal, haven't you heard?
Wouldn't you like to grasp why it is that falling in love
& coming to know, make you feel genuinely
joy's rim? One definition of holiness

places us in the absolute, wedged into sand
spread on the floor where we passed last night, trace
of all that withdraws
& remains.

ii.

Enough the street was a blank sheet
rolling through the Remington, product of tidying
up the room. Did you sleep well?
Did you go to the movies?
That's what all streets are: scribbled
narratives of the workday's end, swallowed
light. When there is nothing to say the light
disappearance exists. The Empire is eternal.
Eternal are the streets. Think of an avenue something less
than sorrow or your love's eyes nothing
like your own, proceeding *x* miles per minute
across a mirror. The water evaporates & only a gaze
remains. Listen to the pages turning.
A tree on the grassy pivot of another surface.
There's a hole in the beam.
The book we're all writing is the fabrication of parallel models
which never meet. In teeth of the typewriter; clouds
plummeting, couch floating on the carpet, your fingers blowing
kisses to the legs.

iii.

Your fingers blowing photographs above my desk.
Out, from here. Nothing's happened, there
are no examples. *So-far* traced by the elm
tree. Through the window I see the leaf. You are the elm
worn on a finger. Here the window scratched
to me. The door bends in front of a field.
The door is the stutter is why. A finite universe;
perverse looking glass. So disposed, the drops suspend
at the tip of each leaf, give off ache to be tucked
in new life. The leaf's vein-of-stem inside each vein
in me, scrapes the window at my desk & I
don't want it. To want is to scrape away time. *Here*
you have the focus of anxiety, of alchemy as where the shadow
sees just how to live: it hovers underneath the feeding
swallow, black on the grassy pivot of another minor
surface. Some of the worst things in your life
never happen.

iv.

Some of the worst things in your life.
This is just an idea & does not occupy space.
As with history, you must admit
oranges were rare & made important gifts,
just as you may soon find in your desk.
Turn the desk around, milky alpha.
The law of love is associated with any.
An orange rolls in a drawer's socket, a universe
flying away from its center. Could be anywhere.
Cross section of an eyeball from which nothing
is released, killed. To believe history, we account
for meaning fleeing meaning a piece of paper
cannot spell. Cables have already been laid to happiness
past & its logistic lines. East is no single point,
irredeemable, beloved. You give your word & it returns
your mouth. To want is to collapse into a gallery of waves
as meanwhile, the holy dread goes on driving.
From between your teeth, the names
are pouring.

SELF-PORTRAITS

(AFTER FRANCESCA WOODMAN)

i.

Let me stand here in the open window I can mock
the dialogue of your hands with rubber gloves
but I only masked the body in the open pane a skin
as though tomorrow ends up no longer like tomorrow
plugged with circles of light from the window
you can see the alley dirty & narrow the body's lines disappearing
or being drawn unevenly dreaming I dreamed of it all comes down to
hands dismantled roundly as though they never existed
careful in syntax & pronunciation the glove
away in the right hand pinning & unpinning
the clothes

ii.

I suppose there is beauty in the way the tape binds
but for the strapping wrapped around my thighs
you woke to find me sitting in this chair & though I
was the subject again the perspective was not mine
I hid my mouth with motion & removed my head
from the frame it was your dream not mine though I was crude
enough to insist on it secretly examining my face in the mirror
& that mouth none of which you can see
only the acre of glove between my legs now chintz
at the window in apartments deep in the ground

iii.

At the window duplicity laying claim a breast
at point blank range black umbrella open
to the question how do you leave behind your, etc.
from hand to mouth the black folds dragging their outlines
& the sound wind moving like truth into a story when making love I can
breathe forever as if there were an answer other
than rain as when you wake next to me & windows slant
around our imageless act within us the text of sex anchored
in the rupture of air thumbs broken from plaiting you
a collar

iv.

A mirror & the things that give such pleasure to the eye but lately I find a sliver of mirror is simply to slice the lid & things are vanishing in time a familiar word passing between us

STUDY FOR SELF-PORTRAITURE

If it had no pencil, would it try mine—now dull & tender
& sweet. If it had no word, would it make the daisy
most as big as I was when it plucked me.
Would those eyes see even less than the tiny nostrils
breathe. Would the penis be slighted, its tip flush
with the contour of thigh if the forearm left
the torso to swing into space, narrow in the grass.
If it came to rest just where you might expect
a signature, would steep rows of white seats swell
for a pencil, a drawing hand. Would the grass divide
as with a comb. Would the penis suggest the conceit of another
pun, for example, genitals = genius, penis = pen
or I'm nobody! Who are you? Would everything work
by repetition, telling each to each: you, you & you.
Would the eye then demand horizon, or more precisely,
would the eye knot & bite its thread. Would it lay an emphatic
thumb with the flutter of something really happening.
Would it be the funeral loose in my body so long it seemed
yesterday across the threshold on the next page.

ORIGIN

The tip of the tongue is free

as it lies upon the body
making entry

Behind its commencement
the spine

a line drawn round
the body

& on a volume of eyeslit
opened

*

The mouth of assembly & vowel

sets interval between us

Readable outline—split

eyeflash broken into air
limb-dissolving

Every utterance becomes a single
instant

underneath blue lid

composition which does not hope
for return

to its origin—

weather hand

*

Your tongue is unknown

resists description

unowned language for which I am obliged
to make myself

a lover with you,
without you, without a
You

STUDY FOR SELF-PORTRAITURE

As to erect the hair, my heart was beating
in the grass. And not only that, but I brought my lounge
to the lawn, my burning chair. I sit, heart beating: one,
one, one. Summers especially I am almost full with small thread
to stitch a red pile, puddles cleared with skiffs;
butterflies searching for sustenance on the meadow
of my body. It is undone business I speak of, this morning,
the blistered welcome stretching from my feet.
In the turn of your book a cloud forms in my neck.
Which is the North which looks North, strict
& blunt. All this or else a life with you, twigs
stacked for bonfire, crows at fishbones
on a vacant lot. Some of you will dress me
as a morning star with flame-proofed paper pompoms,
blue & not yet lit. I will make no decision to look up
or down while a page is described as others
stand pressed against the barbed & galvanized fence
where a seal park barks summer after
summer. Come closer, I'm wearing rubber
boots. I am naked under this poncho! You might want me
in your dress, bowling ball black, pattering
on stones in my own applause.
Maybe you'd like to listen to a good cha-cha?

Drink whiskey? Water the deer?
You might enjoy these grapes held to face or kissing
the bulky shoe. You might want to see a trespassing conch
poised at my ear, a body lying across a shellheap.
I know the quarters of weather, where it comes from,
where it goes. The sea, as I go
out the door, laps like a redness over the floor,
my hair coming down in the middle of a conversation.
When I was resetting the pins, I came to feel the crows
walk on my head as if I were the house.

DOCUMENT PROCESSING

Brute heat rises, weed strong & so carefully I
turn my words about your longing as workers
drag the fallen elm down the driveway.
Fluttering cut from my ear, wanting to copy copy
copy rinds slanting around seed, trunk
& stem. The sound of words I pencil & erase
as the tree's open crown grazes the neighbor's
house, ropes & cuts the scale of ribs below.
In this marvelous disguise of a body,
flies gather at the stump on a pin of light
& sap. I in the form of my own urging, eye
in its movement follows the body's future
path, the sinews of an insect's aggressive
wing twisting white the chainsaw's sugar smoke.
The ear scratched dim among shapes
of the outline, I wear your silence
against the heat. I bring you the disposition
of the double.

HOMAGE TO FRANCESCA WOODMAN

i. Aesthetics: Rome, 1978

Definitions of space by mirrors & windows.

Her hands caress the wall.

In the mirror black brocade opens
to reveal one breast.

A keyboard, brick & raw iron.

The weather is perfect, the sky as blue
as the most exploded tradition fames.

The body, her own body in frame
caught at that point where motion

becomes repose,
a fleeting settling onto paper.

Can you hear the luxury?

Negative impression her prone
body makes

in powder, the impression
of light on silver salts.

ii. New York, East Village, January 1981

She experiences flesh precisely.

Not suffering from any kind of hysterical
numbness, but obstinately

confronts the physical, twenty-two.

Her bed, so close to window.
The open pane of glass

racing in hollows, her knuckles,
arms

holding up her toes sheets flapping
in the wind

where Francesca
Woodman will throw herself
from the twelfth floor.

It's never easy.
Better to laugh.

A verbal narrative would be too complex,
too slow,

would not demonstrate
how our lives

are a charade, conformist
& banal.

iii. Some Disordered Interior Geometries, Detail: 1981

The mirror is a sort of rectangle.
They say mirrors are specified,

specified water. A rectangle is almost a square.
A square created with shutter speed

rolling up her stocking. The mirror
cannot believe its own surface,
water or not, the body's inner force.

She is at this moment
brighter than magnesium ignited.

We cannot say anything about her eyes.

We cannot say anything.

She is also breathing heavily.

She was found naked
trembling with cold, waiting

for the proper exposure.

We are thinking of the tender mouth of the rabbit pulling
at blades of grass. A flower,
if you blink, from bowel to breast.
We want to be so beautiful.
If we wanted, we could remember
anything. The eyes of the rabbit
might be open or closed. There is Friday
& then Saturday. A season changes, years
pass. The long grass lays itself down.
What may be better & what may be
worse & what may be clover
nobody knows. Yes, there is a rabbit on the lawn & the wish
comes true before you make it.
Do you know what you've seen?
Do you know what to do?

FROM THE VELOCITIES

If the Polaroid yellows in time,
not history. If the face is composed
of fourteen bones. The essence, face, the enemy,
arms. If muscle extends the wrist and abducts
the hand, without politic as our engagement.
The index finger can be extended or pointed
while others flex. If the artery is exposed
by making an incision
scattering pigeons. If the city stands on a single finger, a dirty
window. We hang something in its dark little cubes:
the track, the spur & rusty ends of space,
grease. If fingers on the bundled throats of wheat
sweep the fence line, words in a book, a shot.
If action of the muscle is therefore to throw
forearm and hand into position they naturally occupy
when placed across the chest. If our hands, likewise fall
underneath the tree, a pulse in a thumb of a map
composing field. If wind seizes the tree
& ha ha if the heart
lies obliquely in the chest,
a mind which is our being,
wrong & wrong.

45 RPM

Last night I fell from a tree.
It was Tuesday, I woke, a paper wasp drowning
on the nightstand in a glass of water.
Spasms rippled her body until forgive me,
I call it nothing, happened.
You were asleep.
You wouldn't even know what I'm talking about.
I wouldn't even tell you what I know.
The sound of spoons can be heard around the house.
I'm afraid, I'm happy, I love you, I want to eat.
Meanwhile, those little birds are singing
in a language strange to you & me as I watch two
workers load sealed boxes above the slaughter
of glass. The sun is cutting.
In the street, a crate of oranges drops,
breaks.

BALCONY WITH FISH

Three fish lie on a plate
in front of an open window

on the balcony
through which we can see

a path leading to a gate
surrounded by trees.

Linden next to elm next
to chokeberry and so on.

Clouds are swept across the sky.
Today is an apparent day

of empty sleeves & shadows
& red meaning red & red

instead of your finger
painted, ruby-nail, dice

on the point of a needle.
The eye picks, pricks.

Light is failing us,
the white

china & silver earring
& salted herring.

NEW YEAR'S EVE

My window's full of shoreline gone
& gulls slide the glass, suddenly

showing white against the disordered
kelp lashed to a piling at the wharf's

head. Yarrow & sage, bergamot
soaks the postcard, a leaf beetle

arrested in the frame of a postcard
stamp, a barren sky & your Wisconsin

script; field & skyline moving
as the hills slowly do

down invisible tiers
into the sea. Where you are, goldfinches flit

through thistle, slip the margin & grain,
a seedhead unmoors its unorthodox scent:

clover cut & arranged on the sill.
The house is empty.

Here, where burning candles hover
around the border of a porcelain tub, pigeons

on the rooftop turn. A hammer rings
down Henry Street & out the window

a bird is ripped down
by a shot.

SUMMONS

Deer shed metal trucks
on the freeway passing rough lines

of wood, sufficiently tame

I stand in my shoes two shiny graves dogging
my footsteps

feet twisting a stubborn limb

Crossing a field from the opposite
direction of the deer

through the commerce
of a vast continent—

land crammed with intimate
expanses

Cropmarked farmlands, chip
of a nation

Locks unpicked, the West
smells like vinegar

*

Why take refuge in a text
of text

Why deertracks   ahead

to bind this note & break

Voting with my feet
& this hand

Bale square
cloud in my mouth

not politics
the kindling ungathered

*

A series cut
down to dry

leaning against nothing—

clover, rye

The blue shag of the spruce

What will they find with their shovels,
the Americans?

*

The park map weeps

with language glue

provoked by the economics
of hills, galleys, names

that pull thread from their skin

The ridges made from coins
pushed through a narrow
slot

Who fondles the payoff,
finger & shaft

Who fingers the trigger?

*

The movement of pens scratching
our names

Why would I doe
the field

where we cut down trees
filling with snow

The screen blank

The shotgun on the blue screen

coming down on a body
like a body

HIVE

Morning's misguided handle
drafts future in the *flap flap* of geese leaving the lawn.
The face of a calculator counts garbage dumps, drums ink
from the postage meter, drives the earth
in slow waves of cancellation
& street value. Letters resemble bandages.
Bombs resemble human eggs imploding
the imprint of uterine walls. The body lying still
is settling on the shrapnel of oyster
shells in a dream. Shark teeth? The head of a seal?
The dead are to be thrown on rags.
The dead are dull ornaments.
Can the gust of sound from an autopen be scattered
to feed a field of beans, a brood, regime?
Economy writes history. Research papers fall like snow.
Hand writes the shift of social security, counts.
We are all thinking how to describe the mask
of a deity with a big nose or anyone's shoulders.
What good is power if we can't uncoil its awful hair?
Bandages hang like monuments. The grass is pushing up
beneath our feet. Dig in anyone's shadow,
find a turning grave. One pin marking
a honeycombed cell.

ITERATION

Meanwhile, the election season begins
& the Blue Light Special goes public.

Under a black umbrella, our President's marriage carries
a stable freshness up the arrogant steps

of the museum. The rain is perfect,
but a spokesman from the Office of Tourism

has on a gray suit & is always angry. In the rain,
people say things like, I'm afraid of the traffic & laugh

into life beyond themselves.

It's summer now. I turn off the T.V.
I turn off the oven.

Meanwhile, a woman jumps in front of a train.

She was probably drunk & maybe stupid.
Still, I think we owe her some sympathy.

You were undressing. Your head was fire.

PALINODE

i.

In the weeding eye, it can
rain. Sleep.

Yes, comes a measure marked
Spring, between river

& sound, in the speed-up

to spare the number of lakes
in Wisconsin: mallards

flying in the expansion of a singular

disturbance flying nowhere.

Our words stuttering down a ball-
point pen where it snows

& no one can see how
at home I am with my white shoulders.

I built my house to my desire

shaving the outer surface of its urge to wince,
kissing the ache from my lips

that were before winging my hands

tick-tack little wind
strips, without reading, without
speaking.

ii.

Here's the underwater sneak route I found through Bull sluice,
my heart of whip-stitch & trest,

muddy runnels.

Fire on the other side.

The eye-white, sky
of river kissed.

Maybe another way of saying,
I built my house to my desire.

Pines above the shingles.

Star-like, flame,
my hands & the river sluice hinging

an open door or bed.

Simply the river quicker than rock, a house &
the old cracked boat

-hulk, trees where I pass till a star
shows it's gone when it snows.

Eye & knocking heart can bless
the hulk dragging estuary.

The treeline giving way

to only motion, only speech.

HALF-DECEMBER

Winter's lurid buds blast the ice
& junipers pick at embroidery
in mittens, filching snow.

The hand-saw singing not to think
of any misery, pine-

blossom disguising the branches
picking buttons of the dead.

To leave with a tree under your arm
is hazardous

if falling out of sentences the dead make
of your bones.

To leave with a tree is easy if I

curves, steering the wishbone clump
of needles.

This dream the world is having about itself
includes light driving

in our little car, to wave & listen, very bright across
rows.

Will eat the cloud.
Will bind this note, quarrying its margin

toward whatever is there.

Later, more snow pocked with personification
points to the fields, yield

us less a flock browsing the tree

then, sweetheart of whiter walls; your arms
dumb, pluralled.

INTERIOR

In the middle of a tiny spot nearly bare
there is a nice thing to say

that the wrist is leading, cling
peaches slipping from a spoon

for our breakfast, the wrist
leading. I open my eyes again.

The sudden spoon
is the same in no size.

It's barely April on my skin.
Nothing hidden.

A cool rose
rose & pink cut pink

on the table, & a table
means a necessary place

& a revision a revision
of a little thing

where we stand in the kitchen
kissing & I love her

her nipples
pierced, I swear it,

means it does mean
there was a stand

a stand
where it did shake.

OPENING OF A BURR

The owls confined to hunting the freeway's median
suggest we're apt to turn unforgiving points
on ourselves. We skid past them,
the brain dropping letters in falling snow,
picking up speed, breaking into box-
elder. A mantle of snow covers all
of its branches. Mind wired: trunk, appetite,
bird. Each thing ending moves quickly
to the next, a neologism of "never" proving soul is not pathology
but nature & the globe of cranium mere instrument
for gutting fruit, teaching periphery.
What makes the body whittle infinite detail?
The right hand degrades the dress we wear,
dim in the fix of wing. In snow we see corrosively the shape made
by our lives; not the narrative, but this trembling inside
all living—fixed intervals moving space as it muscles
in steps & a cascade of waves below. Our car veers around the handshake,
carrying a wave inside us in the dark.
Little animal life & its habit of hovering,

a hand to repeat oneself in a thousand contexts
until death or irrelevance. A lip by accident. Nest saddled
in a tree. Then, one owl & rodent prey hexed, claimed
where the naked eye catches, thrust,
clinging to its physiology.

ODE

Contained in a cavity
of the Orbit

protected from injury

makes no sequence of event makes
no syllable of Death

Hurries to a sphere & show
& end

loose as a swallow's torso

Wedlock is shyer

Named with a tongue
& repeated

*

Crisis is sweet whiplash
tongue

against the crystalline lens

When the eyelids open
elliptical space

is left between their margins
angles

corresponding to the junction

of upper & lower

Lids

At the commencement

The healed heart shows its shallow
scar

turns your thoughts without a whip

with confidential moan

*

So goes the world
Passes & we stay

The iris & its contractile
curtain

radiating plain as the ego chastened

The sleeping

To wane without disparagement
in the disassembling hue

Size circumscribes, has no room
for petty furniture

or Wedding

The eye in its Orbit
in position to ensure

the most extensive range of sight

Swallows filling an empty
chimney

BULK MECHANICS

i.

When you strike a match to fire
another point fuses the universe
creates scale.

The tongue is the eye

as small as a flashlight carried
in my mouth & then the page

on which nothing happens. Language
is the eye a skirt

rushing North

night of tiny hairs above your lip

the West you were making was never unstoried
or artless, facing disappearance.

Curves catch

on the page like hinges.
A dress with blue sash & then the pulse

where the bird spits

as meanwhile I was famished
in the repetition

of unread messages from here
to what we

call loss.

ii.

Repetition denies being.

The eye breaks

into proposition with an urgency

as my hand would come to seize
you forever.

How does a love end?—Then
does it end?

To tell you the truth, no one—knows
anything a kind of innocence conceals the end
of this thing conceived *lived* according to
eternity.

Still our dream swells, in spite of

& just as I drove nails into that morning
the sight of birds

tore into memory where my heap was calling
yours its own.

What neighborhood?
Only passing & trees or one tree.

Curved a face that there may be speech
of earth, of the flock, my fist
opening floods.

The weather was clear.

Inside & on the surface; empty
the furtive poplar leaf thinking everything
over. That was the echo.

TO A READER

Enough of the body's products
becoming fatal,

too black, too near—in the cake of soap wedding
ring.

The moon cuts thinly at the sink.
A clear spectacle: where is the eye?

I marry into it, mind.
Speed has caught up with speed.
The mind puts the mind by.

No bodies in bodies stand
oppositely.

The eye lags by the moon which singled.
I am not the moon but a singling.

If this be I, torn from a bare cage
of wind, if I my words

am, arguing away herself
by various equations, then also the eye
purifies

as does flying,
debrides a damp brain.

The body then never more a name
without a place to match.

STOLEN FROM A BRANCH

As in the parable, the truant lover
arrived. Morning, not a sample, a quotation,

It was only a bird! but let's forget

about those hidden references touched
by something the *I don't know* that keeps flying

out of your mouth when I'm talking.

To believe or not believe, that is not the question.

Why not the frosty eyelid turning to feathers?

Why not your hand slurred among the sheets
off to educate the woolen peony

of desire, five-fingered glove.

This bed in a bare-walled room, alone
is northern enough

to bend a branch, twist a mind.

In the mind, the sparrow is other, not you
though you also were legislated to fly—

Let's measure the raw, archaic cold

tweezed by chopsticks.
Why not this palace of ice?

Then tears, too, appraised:

a bird stolen from a branch is unforgivable.
In forgiveness, one might easily believe all poems

were about her.

NOTES

"Prayer for Lorine Niedecker"—Niedecker was an essential poet of the Objectivist circle. The three sections of the poem center on classification groups of butterflies and take their titles from the Latin names for these groups: Blues, Sulphurs and Swallowtails.

"Self Portraits (after Francesca Woodman)" & "Homage to Francesca Woodman"—Francesca Woodman (1958–1981) was a photographer who began to take pictures around the age of 13 and pursued her art until her suicide at the age of 22. She was especially interested in self-portraits and often posed in the nude.

"Document Processing"—The title of this poem is stolen from David Rivard.

"Who is her Other a Figure in the Picture Attending"—line 22 adapted from Rae Armantrout.

"45 RPM"—lines 9–10 are from Tomaz Salamun.

"Half December"—lines 1–3 & 6–7 adapted from the opening lines of Richard Meier's poem "Beautiful."

"Summons"—the poem contains language from Lisa Fishman and Mark Levine.

"Opening of a Burr"—"proving soul is not pathology but nature," "Mind wired:" is from Claudia Keelan. "What makes the body whittle infinite detail," is Brenda Shaugnessy.

"Ode"—is for Rachel Moritz.

"Bulk Mechanics"—"Repetition denies being" is Claudia Keelan. "What neighborhood?/...Trees or one tree" is Donald Revell.

"Stolen from a Branch"—the first line in this poem owes a debt to Olga Broumas.

Some of these poems also sample from the following sources; Gertrude Stein's *Tender Buttons*, the letters and poems of Emily Dickinson, the letters of Marcel Proust, *The Golden Book of Birds, Gray's Anatomy* and *Is It Righteous to Be? Interviews with Emmanuel Levinas.* There may be other borrowings in these poems, now lost; I offer my grateful if incomplete acknowledgement.

ABOUT THE AUTHOR

Juliet Patterson's poems have appeared in *American Letters & Commentary, The Bellingham Review, Conduit, Hayden's Ferry Review, Indiana Review, New Orleans Review, Painted Bride Quarterly, Verse* and elsewhere. She lives in Minneapolis and is an adjunct faculty member at the College of Saint Catherine and Hamline University.

ABOUT NIGHTBOAT BOOKS

Nightboat Books, a nonprofit organization, seeks to develop audiences for writers whose work resists convention and transcends boundaries by publishing books rich with poignancy, intelligence, and risk.

The following individuals have supported the publication of this book. We thank them for their generosity and commitment to the mission of Nightboat Books:

Abraham Associates
Craig and Kristen Beddow
Karla Brom
Nick and Suzanne Chapis
Katherine Dimma
Brenda Gold and Dale Wozny
Brian Goldfaden and Nicole DuBois
Joshua Goldfaden
Sarah Heller
Suzanne Heyd
Sharon Jacks and Kevin McDonald
Daniel Lin
James and Carolyn Patterson
Anonymous (1)

Please visit our website at www.nightboat.org to find out how you can support future publications of Nightboat Books.

ALSO AVAILABLE FROM NIGHTBOAT

The Lives of a Spirit / Glasstown: Where Something Got Broken, by Fanny Howe

5 Novels: Nod, Deep North, Famous Questions, Saving History, Indivisible, by Fanny Howe (forthcoming December 2006)

Nightboat Books is committed to preserving ancient forests and natural resources. We elected to print *The Truant Lover* on 50% post consumer recycled paper, processed chlorine free. As a result, for this printing, we have saved:

3 trees (40' tall and 6-8" diameter)
1,259 gallons of water
506 kilowatt hours of electricity
139 pounds of solid waste
273 pounds of greenhouse gases

Nightboat Books made this paper choice because our printer, Thomson-Shore, Inc., is a member of Green Press Initiative, a nonprofit program dedicated to supporting authors, publishers, and suppliers in their efforts to reduce their use of fiber obtained from endangered forests.

For more information, visit www.greenpressinitiative.org